END OF AN ERA

Photo memories of Manchester City at Maine Road

Richard Tucker

HALSGROVE

First published in Great Britain in 2011

Copyright © Richard Tucker

British Library Cataloguing-in-Publication Data
A CIP record for this title is available from the British Library

ISBN 978 0 85704 123 4

HALSGROVE
Halsgrove House,
Ryelands Business Park,
Bagley Road, Wellington, Somerset TA21 9PZ
Tel: 01823 653777   Fax: 01823 216796
email: sales@halsgrove.com

Part of the Halsgrove group of companies
Information on all Halsgrove titles is available at: www.halsgrove.com

Printed in Italy by Grafiche Flaminia

THE END OF AN ERA

Supporting City over the years has been a roller-coaster affair. There have been highs and lows and plenty of memories. In the early days I used to cycle to Maine Road and leave the bike in one of the local houses near the ground. Standing on the Kippax required an early start as it was better and safer if you stood behind or just in front of one of the barriers. Otherwise when a home goal was scored there was always a danger of falling when the crowd surged forward. You often ended up yards from where you started! Modern Health and Safety Officers would have been appalled! If you were late for a big game it was a question of jumping up and down at the back of the Kippax just to get a view of the ball in the air. The gates were normally opened twenty minutes from the end so there were quite a few 'latecomers'. Kids were often on the shoulders of fathers or held on top of the barriers. They were also lifted shoulder high down to the front on many occasions. I have sat or stood in all parts of the ground over the years. Starting in the upper section of the Platt Lane corner Stand I then spent some time at the back of the Main Stand in the early fifties and also stood in both North and South Stands. After my return from Hong Kong I also had the opportunity to sit in the press box on several occasions covering games for the Hong Kong *Tiger Standard* as their overseas sports writer. The Kippax Stand however was my main watching area and in games when there wasn't a large crowd you were able to easily move from one end to the other to see City score! When the Kippax Stand changed into an all seater in 1995 I remember queuing for hours in order to get a front row seat in the upper tier. To their credit when Eastlands took over from Maine Road the club made sure supporters kept similar seats in the new stadium.

MAINE RD

Well I have seen off nearly thirty managers since I started watching City and used about 15 different film and digital cameras over the years to snap memories both good and bad of games following the club.

There have been periods when other football and work commitments both home and abroad have kept me away

from Maine Road but hopefully you will enjoy viewing images of games and players that will bring back memories. There are over 200 pictures from 48 games in the book and many of the original negatives and trannies required plenty of tender loving care and attention in Photoshop to enable them to be used.

You will find lots more on my many City web pages –
www.rtfract.com
www.rtfract.com/rtcity.htm
www.mancity.tk

Finally it's thanks to City author extraordinaire Gary James for his help.

In the early days there were no such things as loyalty points – though tokens helped later on – you just had to queue, sometimes for many hours, in order to buy a ticket. I can remember getting to Maine Road early on a Sunday morning and not getting a ticket until well into the afternoon. Queues to get through the turnstiles on match days were often controlled by police on horseback and there were many attempts by supporters to climb over the wall!

After the war United also used Maine Road until the 1949-50 season. Their ground had been bombed during the war and like many supporters starved of football during the war years I watched both United and City at Maine Road. So I was able to be at the United Arsenal game on 17 Jan 1948 when 83,260 were packed into Maine Road. The game ended 1-1 with Jack Rowley (for United) and Lewis (for Arsenal) scoring. Among the Arsenal players were Leslie Compton and Joe Mercer. About this time both Manchester teams often attracted crowds of over 50 or 60 thousand. The highest City home crowd I witnessed was just after Christmas in 1957 when City drew with United 2 all. Almost 70,500 saw Joe Hayes and an own goal by Foulkes cancel out goals by Denis Violett and Bobby Charlton.

As for memorable games involving City there were many. One of the earliest I can remember was important for several reasons. It took place on 14 June 1947, the season's latest finish in City's history. City beat Newport County 5-1 and became champions of Division Two while Newport County were relegated having conceded 133 goals in 42 games – a record since the war. George Smith scored all five goals for City and it was the debut of Roy Clarke the Welsh left winger. It was also the last game for Sam Barkas and Maurice Dunkley. That same season in April City played a friendly game against Glasgow Rangers and I remember that game for one reason only – the visiting supporters. Before then we had never seen such passion complete with banners and flags etc. Thousands had travelled down from Scotland. City won 2-1 with goals from Alec Herd and George Smith. In those days it was rare enough to see any visiting supporters let alone many coach loads. Segregation did not come in for many years.

I don't have too many happy memories of away games having witnessed City being well beaten at Derby County 7 nil on a mud heap in pouring rain and Bert Trautmann was in goal – his third game! That was in December 1949.

Another disappointing day out was at the end of the 1962-63 season. I had been given tickets by Cliff Sear our left back to watch City's game at West Ham hoping we could avenge our home 1-6 defeat (Trautmann had been sent off, Alan Oakes playing in goal). Alas we got beaten 6-1 again and were relegated.

Easily one of the best memories was at the end of the 1967-68 season when I drove to Newcastle to see City win 4-3 It was an exciting game and the A1 was a mass of blue and 20,000 City supporters probably outnumbered the home fans. Goals by Neil Young 2, Lee and Summerbee ensured City won the First Division two points clear of United who had been beaten at home by Sunderland.

A year later and this time it was a trip down south to see City play at Wembley in the Cup Final against Leicester City. I had visited Wembley several times previously both as a steward and in the press box but this was the first time to see City. A great day out was made all the better by Neil Young's winning goal. It was a great end to a rather indifferent season.

I have witnessed some high scores but the 10-1 slaughter of Huddesfield Town in November 1987 takes some beating. There were three hat-tricks that day from Adcock, Stewart and White. The crowd – only 20,000 alas – were shouting for more and more after City had scored six and time ran out before the team could manage eleven!

The Division Two play-off game against Gillingham at Wembley in 1999 will be remembered for ever by all who witnessed it. It was a remarkable recovery by City who went two down with just 4 minutes to go. Many City fans had left when City equalized in added time. Winning the penalty shoot-out was so important. If City had remained in Division Two who knows what would have happened! City went on to gain promotion to the Premiership and now they are one of the richest clubs in the world.

City v Chelsea 1-1 September 1954

Trautmann takes a cross with ease.

Trautmann, Meadows, Little, Barnes, Ewing, Paul, Fagan, McAdams, Revie, Hart, Clark.
Robertson, Harris, Willemse, Armstrong, Greenwood, Saunders, Parsons, McNichol, Bentley, Stubbs, Lewis.

Robertson saves from Johnny Hart (far right on the ground). Note the position of the linesman. Don Revie is just below the ball.

Bentley scores for Chelsea. Roy Paul had scored for City.

Robertson in the Chelsea goal waits for a City shot.

City v Tottenham Hotspur 4-1 December 1967

The famous 'Ballet on Ice' game – Jimmy Greaves scoring for Spurs.

*Mulhearn, Book, Pardoe, Doyle, Heslop, Oakes, Lee, Bell, Summerbee, Young, Coleman.
Jennings, Kinnear, Knowles, Mullery, Hoy, Mackay, Saul, Greaves, Gilzean, Venables, Jones.*

The 'Ballet on Ice' game – Doyle heads clear.

City v Leicester City 1-0 Cup Final, April 1969

LEICESTER CITY
(Royal Blue Shirts, White Shorts)

1. P. SHILTON
2. P. RODRIGUES
3. D. NISH (Captain)
4. R. ROBERTS
5. J. SJOBERG
6. G. CROSS
7. R. FERN
8. D. GIBSON
9. A. LOCHHEAD
10. A. CLARKE
11. L. GLOVER

Substitute: M. MANLEY

Manager: Mr. F. O'FARRELL

Trainer: Mr. M. Musgrove

FOOTBALL ASSOCIATION CHALLENGE CUP COMPETITION

FINAL

Leicester City
v
Manchester City

SATURDAY 26th APRIL 1969 Kick-Off 3pm

EMPIRE STADIUM WEMBLEY. Official Programme 2/-

REFEREE
G. McCABE
(Sheffield and Hallamshire)

Today's match brings both the climax and the finale to the refereeing career of Mr. George McCabe, because this is his season of retirement from the Football League list on reaching the age of 47. He took up refereeing in India and Burma during the war while a registered player with Sheffield Wednesday.

Mr. McCabe, a Company Director, was appointed to the full Football League list in 1953 (after three years as a linesman) and to the F.I.F.A. panel in 1960 and has officiated at big games throughout the world. He has a permanent reminder of World Cup appointments, as both referee and linesman at his home in Sheffield as he has named his house 'Jules Rimet'.

LINESMEN
K. H. BURNS
(Birmingham)
F. C. LANE
(Sussex)

MANCHESTER CITY
(Red/Black Striped Shirts, Black Shorts)

1. H. DOWD
2. A. BOOK (Captain)
3. G. PARDOE
4. M. DOYLE
5. T. BOOTH
6. A. OAKES
7. M. SUMMERBEE
8. C. BELL
9. F. LEE
10. N. YOUNG
11. A. COLEMAN

Substitute: D. CONNOR

Manager: Mr. J. MERCER

Trainer: Mr. D. Ewing

To reach the final City beat Luton 1-0, Newcastle United 2-0 (replay), Blackburn Rovers 4-1, Spurs 1-0, and Everton 1-0 in the semi-final at Villa Park.

Part of the 100,000 crowd making their way down Wembley Way from the tube station.

City hat choice.

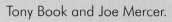

Wembley Way.

City coach on its way.

Tony Book and Joe Mercer.

The teams are presented to Princess Anne.

Neil Young shoots for goal.

City players appeal for offside.

Shilton saves – watched by Bell and Lee.

Shilton saves under pressure from Bell.

Harry Dowd saves by the post.

Neil Young scores the winning goal for City beating Shilton.

City celebrate after Young's goal.

Malcolm Allison shows the FA Cup to the crowd.

Colin Bell and Alan Oakes carry the FA Cup.

One of City's greatest supporters Helen Turner who recently passed away aged 85 is in the centre of the three seated ladies in Albert Square waiting for the team to arrive.

Joe Mercer.

Francis Lee.

Joe Mercer laughs at Malcolm Allison.

Malcolm Allison with the cup.

Malcolm Allison celebrates watched by Tommy Booth.

City v Stoke City 4-1 September 1970

Tony Book shoots and scores to open the scoring.

Tony Book celebrates a rare goal for him in City's fifth win on the run.

Neil Young scores past Gordon Banks.

Young celebrates.

Mike Summerbee on a run.

Corrigan, Book, Pardoe, Doyle, Booth, Oakes, Summerbee, Bell, Lee, Young, Towers.

Young about to centre.

Stoke under pressure.

Banks saves from Summerbee.

Banks punches clear.

The New Kippax Stand Under Construction 1995

The famous Kippax Stand at Maine Road is here undergoing major surgery as a result of the Taylor Report following the Hillsborough disaster. Work is continuing on the upper level as the crowd enjoy sitting for the first time in the lower level.

City v Tottenham Hotspur 0-1 May 1971

The roof to cover the North Stand under construction.

Francis Lee shoots for goal.

Healey, Book, Connor, Towers, Heslop, Donachie, Mellor, Hill, Lee, Young, Bowyer.

Pat Jennings catches a corner under pressure from George Heslop.

City v Burnley 0-1 August 1973 Charity Shield

Francis Lee with the ball – other City players are Marsh and Law.

Corrigan, Book, Donachie, Doyle, Booth, Oakes, Summerbee, Bell, Law, Lee, Marsh.

This was the last Charity Shield Final played on a club ground.

Rodney Marsh about to shoot.

Denis Law tries to beat a defender watched by Colin Bell.

Tommy Booth heads clear.

City v Ipswich Town 1-3 April 1974

Denis Tueart celebrates as a Summerbee header beats the keeper.

MacRea, Pardoe, Donachie, Doyle, Barrett, Horswill, Summerbee, Bell, Carrodus, Oakes, Tueart.

City v Norwich City 4-0 September 1977

Mike Channon makes a goal for Asa Hartford.

Corrigan, Clements, Donachie, Owen, Watson, Booth, Barnes, Channon, Kidd, Hartford, Power.

Peter Barnes in action.

City v Bristol City 2-0 May 1979

City take a free kick.

Corrigan, Reid, Donachie, Henry, Watson, Bell, Channon, Deyna, Silkman, Hartford, Power.

Joe Corrigan punches clear.

Corrigan waits to save.

Asa Hartford centres. Notice Gerry Gow in the background. He was later to play for City.

Channon goes up with the keeper as he punches clear.

City v Everton 3-1 April 1981

Denis Tueart breaks through.

Mackenzie tries to score.

Corrigan, Henry, McDonald. Reid, Power, Booth, Bennett, Tueart, MacKenzie, Buckley, Sugrue.

Notice a young Gary Megson (next to Tueart) playing for Everton.

Paul Power takes a corner against Everton.

Paul Power takes yet another corner – different game!

Denis Tueart in action.

Corrigan, Ranson, McDonald, Reid, Power, Caton, Tueart, Henry, McKenzie, Hutchinson, Reeves.

Brighton defend a corner.

City v Manchester United 0-3 February 1995

Peter Schmeichel saves under pressure from Rosler.

Dibble, Summerbee, D. Brightwell, Kernaghan, Curle, I.Brightwell, Gaudino, Walsh, Rosler, Flitcroft, Beagrie.

Andrei Kanchelskis tries to beat Kernaghan watched by Ince, Beagrie and Flitcroft.

City v Tottenham Hotspur 1-1 August 1995

Immel on his debut in goal for City catches under pressure.

Immel, Edghill, Phelan, Lomas, Symonds, I. Brightwell, N. Summerbee, Walsh, Rosler, Flitcroft, Kinkladze.

Richard Edghill clears from Sheringham.

Paul Walsh in a heading dual.

Uwe Rosler – one of City's favourites – tries to break through.

City supporters show their appreciation to Uwe Rosler on scoring.

Niall Quinn scores with a header.

Srnicek saves from Nicky Summerbee.

Cult player Georgi Kinkladze tries to outfox four defenders.

Immel, Summerbee, Hiley, Curle, Symons, Lomas, Brown, Clough, Rosler, Quinn, Kinkladze.

Kevin Horlock scores the second goal.

Substitute Allsop is about to beat the keeper to make it four nil.

York keeper Mimms punches clear under pressure from Taylor.

Weaver, Edghill, Crooks, Wiekens, Horlock, Vaughan, Brown, Bishop, Dickov, Taylor, Cooke.

City v Gillingham 2-2 City Won 3-1 on Penalties May 1999 Division 2 Promotion Play-off at Wembley

Having finished third in the Second Division it was vital that City achieved promotion so the situation looked dire with just 4 minutes to go City were two down to Gillingham. City looked dead and buried. As full time approached Kevin Horlock scored to give the remaining City supporters hope. After almost five minutes of added time Paul Dickov shot past Bartram to level the scores. City supporters who had left early tried desperately to get back into the ground for the 30 minutes extra time which ended goal-less. We then had the dramatic penalty shoot-out.

Horlock scores for City 1-0

Nicky Weaver saves from Smith – still 1-0

Paul Dickov hits the post – still 1-0

Pennock misses for Gillingham – still 1-0

Terry Cooke scores for City – 2-0

Hodge scores for Gillingham – 2-1

Edgehill scores for City – 3-1

Weaver saves from Butters and City are promoted

Weaver, Crooks (Taylor), Edghill, Wiekens, Morrison (Vaughan), Horlock, Brown (Bishop), Whitley, Dickov, Goater, Cooke.

City v Wolverhampton Wanderers 0-1 August 1999

Nicky Weaver saves from Dean.

Wolves keeper Stowell makes a great save from a Morrison header.

Weaver, Edghill, Granville, Wiekens, Morrison, Horlock, Cooke, Whitley, Dickov, Goater, Kennedy.

City v Sheffield United 6-0 August 1999

Kevin Horlock scores from the spot following a handball offence in the area.

Shaun Goater is brought down just outside the penalty area and Sheffield United keeper Simon Tracy gets a red card.

Weaver, Edghill, Tiatto, Wiekens, Morrison, Horlock, Cooke, Whitley, Dickov, Goater, Kennedy.

Shaun Goater scores with a header from a pass from Cooke to make it 4-0.

Gareth Taylor scores City's 6th goal following a pass from Kennedy.

City v Grimsby Town 2-1 December 1999

Peacock attempts a header at a City corner.

Weaver, Edghill, Granville, Wiekens, Jobson, Horlock, Bishop, Pollock, Goater, Peacock, Tiatto.

Shaun Goater scores with a volley from a pass from Ian Bishop.

Weaver, Edghill, Tiatto, Wiekens, Jobson, Pollock, Bishop, Whitley, Taylor, Goater, Kennedy.

Spencer Prior scores his first goal for City following his transfer from Derby.

Weaver, Edghill, Tiatto, Prior, Jobson, Horlock, Wiekens, Whitley, Dickov, Goater, Kennedy.

Weaver, Edghill, Tiatto, Prior, Jobson, Horlock, Wiekens, Whitley, Taylor, Goater, Kennedy.

Robert Taylor forces the ball home past Myhre to win the game for City.

The celebrations start.

Despite several Tannoy announcements there was a pitch invasion on the final whistle to celebrate the end of the season and almost certain promotion to the Premiership.

George Weah crosses for Wanchope to score and open the scoring. Wanchope went on to score a hat-trick.

Haaland scores City's second from a cross from Wanchope.

Weaver, Edghill, Tiatto, Prior, Howey, Horlock, Wiekens, Haaland, Wanchope, Weah, Kennedy.

City v Coventry City 1-2 August 2000

The two benches with managers Joe Royle (City) and Gordon Strachan (Coventry).

Weaver, Edghill, Tiatto, Prior, Howey, Horlock, Wiekens, Haaland, Wanchope, Weah, Kennedy.

Silver-booted George Weah's shot is brilliantly saved by Hedman.

Hedman blocks Wanchope's shot but Horlock scores from the rebound.

The open 'Gene Kelly' stand.

Middlesbrough defend a City corner.

Weaver, Haaland, Ritchie, Prior, Howey, Horlock, Wiekens, Whitley, Wanchope, Weah, Kennedy.

City v Newcastle United 0-1 September 2000

City keeper Tommy Wright saving from Alan Shearer. It was both Wright's and Weah's last game for City.

Wright, Haaland, Tiatto, Prior, Richie, Horlock, Wiekens, Whitley, Wanchope, Weah, Dickov.

City v Bradford City 2-0 October 2000

A Haaland free kick is deflected past the Bradford keeper for City's second goal.

Weaver, Haaland, Ritchie, Prior, Howey, Tiatto, Wiekens, Whitley, Wanchope, Dickov, Kennedy.

City v Manchester United 0-1 November 2000

Referee Dunn tries to sort out a problem. He'd better hurry up – Roy Keane is on his way over!

Weaver, Charvet, Tiatto, Prior, Howey, Haaland. Wiekens, Whitley, Dickov, Wright-Phillips, Kennedy.

David Beckham about to take a free kick.

Weaver saves from Scholes.

Paul Dickov has a word with Garry Neville.

City v Everton 5-0 December 2000

Wanchope scores for City as Gerrard parries a Horlock free kick.

Weaver, Charvet, Tiatto, Dunne, Howey, Horlock, Haaland, Whitley, Wanchope, Goater, Wright-Phillips.

City v Tottenham Hotspur 0-1 February 2001

An indirect free kick inside the penalty area is unusual nowadays. Note that the Spurs players were moving before the ball was kicked! There was no replay of the free kick.

Weaver, Weikens, Granville, Dunne, Howey, Haaland, Kanchelskis, Whitley, Huckerby, Goater, Tiatto.

Andy Morrison scores with a header from a corner.

Weaver, Edghill, Granville, Dunne, Howey, Morrison, Wiekens, Haaland, Huckerby, Goater, Tiatto.

Shaun Goater scores from a penalty after Haaland was brought down.

City v Watford 3-0 August 2001

A great display by City to start their season in Division One under new manager Kevin Keegan. Pearce and Berkovic made their debuts.

Nash, Charvet, Granville, Dunne, Howey, Pearce, Wiekens, Berkovic, Wanchope, Goater, Tiatto.

Goater scores City's first with a header.

A Stuart Pearce free kick makes it 3 nil for City.

City v Crewe Alexandra 5-2 August 2001

The referee turns down a City shout for a penalty.

Weaver, Chauvet, Granville, Dunne, Howey, Pearce, Wiekens, Wright-Phillips, Wanchope, Goater, Tiatto.

Stuart Pearce scores from a penalty following a hand ball offence.

City v Birmingham City 3-0 September 2001

The minute's silence before the game was impeccably observed in memory of the events of 9/11 in New York.

Weaver, Edghill, Granville, Dunne, Howey, Pearce, Benarbia, Etuhu, Wanchope, Goater, Tiatto.

Ali Benarbia and Dickson Etuhu made their debuts.

Richard Dunne scores his first goal for City.

Goater scores for City from a corner by Pearce.

City v Walsall 3-0 September 2001

Ali Benarbia – signed on a free transfer from Paris St-Germain – was one of the most creative players ever to play for City. Alas he arrived towards the end of his career but he soon became a firm favourite with the fans.

Paulo Wanchope scored from the spot for City's third goal.

Weaver, Wiekens, Granville, Dunne, Howey, Pearce, Benarbia, Etuhu, Wanchope, Goater, Tiatto.

City v Rotherham United 2-1 November 2001

Negouai scores following a corner and good work by Pearce and Benarbia but the Rotherham players disputed the goal claiming it was handled. It was Leon Mike's (32) only full appearance for City.

Weaver, Dunne, Tiatto, Mettomo, Howey, Pearce, Benarbia, Negouai, Huckerby, Mike, Wright-Phillips.

City v Burnley 5-1 December 2001

Carlo Nash saves a penalty from Little.

Kevin Horlock heads off the line a shot from Ball.

Nash, Edghill, Tiatto, Mettomo, Howey, Weikens, Benarbia, Berkovic, Wanchope, Goater, Horlock.

Just before half time Paulo Wanchope completed a well-deserved hat-trick after great work by Berkovic.

City keeper Carlo Nash makes a great save from ex-City player Gareth Taylor.

City v Norwich City 3-1 January 2002

Down to ten men (Tiatto sent off after ten minutes) Berkovic scored City's first goal.

Paulo Wanchope scores from a penalty after keeper Green had brought down Goater.

Berkovic scores a wonderful solo goal after a run from the half-way line and he celebrates below.

Nash, Wright-Phillips, Tiatto, Dunne, Howey, Wiekens, Benarbia, Berkovic, Wanchope, Goater, Horlock.

City v Barnsley 5-1 April 2002

The ball is just about to cross the line to give City their 99th goal of the season. Huckerby was the scorer following good work by Benarbia and Macken.

Nash, Wright-Phillips, Jensen, Dunne, Howey , Pearce, Benarbia, Horlock, Huckerby, Macken, Tiatto.

Jenson passes to the unmarked Macken who scores City's 100th goal of the season.

Macken scores his second goal and City's fifth.

City v Portsmouth 3-1 April 2002

Steve Howey heads an early goal past Dave Beasant for City.

Stuart Pearce in his final game fails from the penalty spot.

Nash, Wright-Phillips, Jensen, Dunne , Howey , Pearce, Benarbia, Horlock, Huckerby, Goater, Tiatto.

City under Keegan win the league and promotion to the Premiership.

City v Manchester United 3-1 November 2002

A run by Anelka gave Goater a chance. His shot was parried by Barthez…

… straight to Anelka who scores after 6 minutes.

Peter Schmeichel saves at the feet of van Nistelrooy. This was the last 'derby' game at Maine Road and Peter Schmeichel was only the second player who had played for both City and United to captain the side – Billy Meridith being the other. It was the very first time there were no Englishmen in the City starting eleven!

Schmeichel, Sun, Mettomo, Dunne, Wiekens, Foe, Jensen, Berkovic, Tiatto, Annelka, Goater. Barthez, G.Neville, P. Neville, Veron, Blanc, Ferdinand, Sylvestre, Scholes, Giggs, Solskjaer, van Nistelrooy.

After 25 minutes a long ball from Foe looked like going out of play. Garry Neville was shepherding the ball out when he was robbed by Shaun Goater who hammered the ball past Barthez for City's second goal. It was Goater's 99th goal for City. He later scored his 100th.

City v Aston Villa 3-1 December 2002

Substitute Ali Benarbia throws himself forward to score.

Marc-Vivian Foe scores City's third goal from a good pass from Benarbia.

Schmeichel, Wright-Phillips, Tiatto, Dunne, Howey, Distin, Foe, Berkovic, Anelka, Goater, Horlock.

City v Liverpool 0-1 FA Cup January 2003

Kirkland punches away a Benarbia free kick.

Schmeichel, Jihai, Jensen, Mettomo, Wiekens, Distin, Benarbia, Foe, Anelka, Wright-Phillips, Horlock.

Schmeichel goes up for a corner in the final moments.

One of the last moments in the last FA Cup tie at Maine Road – Schmeichel heading clear!

City v Fulham 4-1 January 2003

Taking a great pass from Benarbia, Anelka shoots between Taylor's legs to level the scores.

Foe made it 3-1 after Taylor had parried his header.

Nash, Sommeil, Howey, Distin, Dunne, Benarbia, Foe, Horlock, Jensen, Belmadi, Anelka.

City v Middlesbrough 0-0 April 2003

Watched by one of City's greatest fans colourful Helen Turner (top left) Peter Schmeichel saves from Job in the opening seconds.

City v Sunderland 3-0 April 2003

Foe scoring for City after a run by Anelka down the right wing.

Schmeichel, Dunne, Distin, Sommeil, Jensen, Foe, Barton, Wright-Phillips, Benarbia, Anelka, Fowler.

This was the very last City goal at Maine Road and it was scored by No. 23 Marc-Vivien Foe who died tragically a few months later from a heart-related illness in the middle of a game between Cameroon and Colombia. The No. 23 shirt has been withdrawn from use. Foe played 38 times for City and scored 9 goals.

The Final Game at Maine Road – City v Southampton 0-1 May 11th 2003

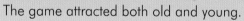
The game attracted both old and young.

A quick snack before the game.

A window display in one of the local houses.

The Blue Moon Chippy.

Denis Law gives the thumbs up.

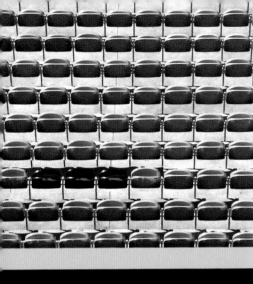

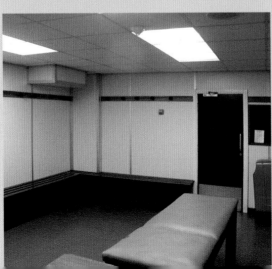

Trophy cabinets.

The 'golden oldies' meet up before the game. See who you can spot!

Maine Road - 'End of an Era'

Anelka beats keeper Jones but fails to score.

Schmeichel saves.

Jones saves for Southampton.

Last ever goal scored – Svensson heads past Schmeichel.

Southampton manage to clear a City corner.

Peter Schmeichel's last save of his career.

Fowler jumps over Jones in the last action of the game .

The goal posts are removed for the very last time.

The players say farewell to the fans.

The team: *Schmeichel, Sommeil, Dunne, Distin, Jensen, Wright-Phillips, Benarbia, Foe, Barton, Goater, Anelka.*

The post match entertainment starts.

"They said it was all over - it is now"

Maine Road February 2010

The 2010-2011 season saw City finish third in the Premiership and qualify for the Champions League. City also won the Cup Final against Stoke City, their first bit of silverware for many years.

Will this be the start of a new era for City fans?